DATE DUE

JY 25 '92	JAN 20 '9	OCT 19 '9	NO 02 '00
AG 5 '92	JUL 31 '9	AT 03 '99	NR 27 '02
AG 12 '92	SEP 02 '9	JE 29 '9	AG 19 '02
SE 8 '92	OCT 01 '9	OC 25 '99	OC 5 '02
SE 25 '92	NOV 19 '9	NO 15 '00	
NO 27 '92	APR 27 '9	DE 11 '99	MR 01 '04
FE 17 '93	JUL 08 '9	FE 19 '0	OC 03 '08
	JUL 15 '9	AP 06 '00	
OC 7 '93			
OCT 14 '94	JUL 29 '9		
APR 10 '96	AUG 17 '9	JE 2 '00	
OCT 31 '96	SEP 18 '9	AG 19 '00	
DEC 04 '96	SEP 28 '9	OC 10 '00	
		DE 08 '00	
		MY 07 '0	
		NO 04 '02	
		DE 17 '07	
		MY 14 '08	

Action
Skateboarding

Action
Skateboarding

Jan Andrejtschitsch, Raimund Kallée & Petra Schmidt

Sterling Publishing Co., Inc.   New York

Photo Credits

J. Andrejtschitsch: pages 28, 29, 30, 33, 34/35, 36/37, 38/39, 42/43,
44/45, 46/47, 48/49, 50, 51 top, 55 bottom, 58/59, 66/67, 68/69,
70/71, 72, 76/77, 78/79, 82/83, 84/85, 86/87, 88/89, 92, 93, 94/95,
96/97, 98 top and bottom, 100, 101, 102/103, 104/105, 106, 108/109,
110/111, 112/113, 114/115, 116/117, 118/119
Kalak/Böhm Bildarchiv: pages 2/3, 8, 13, 27, 56, 60/61, 62/63, 64, 65,
73, 80, 81, 89 top, 99, 107, 120/121
R. Kallée: pages 10, 14/15, 19, 22, 26, 51 bottom, 74/75, 90, 91,
98 center
P. Schmidt: pages 17, 18, 21, 23, 24, 25, 32, 40/41, 52/53, 54/56
T. Salomon: page 35 top
Cover Photo: Kalak/Böhm Bildarchiv (front), Karin Staab (back)
Layout: Manfred Sinicki

Translated by Elisabeth E. Reinersmann

Library of Congress Cataloging-in-Publication Data

Andrejtschitsch, Jan.
    [Skateboarding know-how. English]
    Action skateboarding / Jan Andrejtschitsch, Raimund Kallée & Petra
Schmidt ; [translated by Elisabeth E. Reinersmann].
        p.   cm.
    Translation of: Skateboarding know-how.
    Includes index.
    Summary: Discusses the history, equipment, and techniques of
skateboarding, examining such styles as streetstyle, halfpipe or
vertical, and freestyle.
    ISBN 0-8069-8500-3
    1. Skateboarding — Juvenile literature.   [1. Skateboarding.]
I. Kallée, Raimund.   II. Schmidt, Petra.   III. Title.
GV859.8.A5313   1992
796.2'1 — dc20   91-40328
                                                       CIP
                                                        AC

10 9 8 7 6 5 4 3 2 1

English translation © 1992 by Sterling Publishing Company
387 Park Avenue South, New York, N.Y. 10016
Original edition published under the title
Skateboarding Know-how © 1991 by BLV Verlagsgesellschaft mbH, Munich
Distributed in Canada by Sterling Publishing
% Canadian Manda Group, P.O. Box 920, Station U
Toronto, Ontario, Canada M8Z 5P9
Distributed in Great Britain and Europe by Cassell PLC
Villiers House, 41/47 Strand, London WC2N 5JE
Distributed in Australia by Capricorn Link Ltd.
P.O. Box 665, Lane Cove, NSW 2066
Printed in Hong Kong
All rights reserved

Sterling ISBN 0-8069-8500-3 Trade
            0-8069-8501-1 Paper

PREFACE

Skateboarding has been experiencing a boom the extent of which has been duplicated by very few other sports. In ever increasing numbers, young people have become fascinated by it and are dedicating their lives, or at least a vast portion of their free time, to this activity. But skateboarding is by no means appreciated by kids alone. Over recent years, it has grown and developed into a serious and competitive sport with all the usual components: professionalism, international contests, and a sizeable industry. However, when taken as part of the general sports world, skateboarding remains understandably an isolated sport, making do without a representative organization, official system of trainers, and even without an established concept of training as such.

Skateboarding thrives on the ideas and efforts of the individual skaters themselves.

This book, therefore, is not to be viewed as an instruction manual. Rather it is an attempt by the authors to shed some light on the sport, give beginning enthusiasts a "leg up," and offer tips and encouragement to those skaters who are ready to leave the "game" behind and take up the sport of skateboarding in earnest.

The authors felt it important, however, to describe the individual maneuvers as a guide to performance, not merely put captions to pictures as is often done in magazines and books. We also attempted to point out the degree of difficulty involved in learning and executing the various tricks and alert the reader to the mistakes frequently made during the learning process, suggesting ways to avoid them.

Just as there are many paths to reaching a goal, there is no one way to perform a skateboarding trick; rather there are many variations on how a stunt can be accomplished. Besides, a skater will learn very quickly what works and what doesn't, and what has to be changed when something has gone wrong.

Allow us, at this point, to express our thanks to those who made this book possible. First and foremost, we want to thank Jamie Luker for his never-ending patience and his never-wavering enthusiasm for the sport of skateboarding.

The following skaters are represented in the photographs: Stefan Lehnert, Alex Philpott, Patrick Meunacher. Special mention goes to Flo-rian Böhm who, in spite of an almost unbearable heat wave, performed outstanding examples of skateboarding, presenting himself and his professionalism in the very best light — thank you, Florian! Last, but not least, we would like to thank the Bad Company for their kind support. A very special thanks, too, goes to Bernie Radwan. His help was indispensable, not only in his role as a skater but also for his contribution to the "street-style" portion of this book.

Jan Andrejtschitsch
Raimund Kallée
Petra Schmidt

CONTENTS

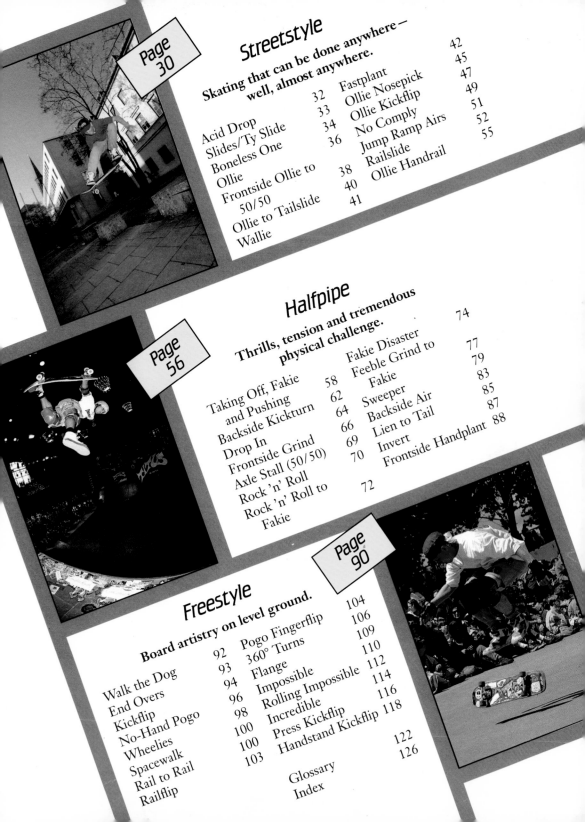

Why don't they run after and kick a ball? Why not try to hit a ball with a bat? How about trying to run a distance that is considered difficult even on a bicycle and which took the life of the first person who ever ran it? Maybe these people think they can make money without getting into tennis? Or they don't really feel like running through a strange town in their shorts in the company of thousands of others? Or maybe they prefer the noise of street traffic to the quiet and calm of a golf course? Granted, these responses do not quite satisfy, and it would be a disservice to skateboarding if its appeal is measured only by comparing it to other types of sport activities. What, then, gives skateboarding its fascinating appeal, and what compels particularly young people to step on the board?

Skateboarding is not only a sport, it is also a means of getting from one place

INTRODUCTION

Why would anyone want to take up skateboarding?

to another. Too, as trite as it might sound and more than anything else, it is a way of expressing an attitude towards life.

But let's talk first about the sport itself. Skateboarding is comprised of three distinct disciplines: Freestyle, street-style, and vertical skating. Each makes specific demands on the skater, physically as well as mentally, and, therefore, appeals to different tastes. Freestyle demands a good feeling for the board and a certain amount of fine motor skills; while the vertical skater, in the half-pipe, needs conditioning and an excellent sense of balance. Freestyle is a discipline for individualists primarily interested in concentrating on their boards and themselves; while street-style and vertical

skating are group activities that appeal to those who thrive on competition. In spite of these differences, all three disciplines have one thing in common: skateboarding is a constant learning process. In this sense it is somewhat special. Contrary to almost all other sports, skateboarding does not distinguish between training and practical application. A skater does not learn something that is then constantly repeated; rather, the accumulative effect of mastering many different tricks forces the skater to be alert to ever new challenges and risks. A skateboarder will never be bored. The opportunity to constantly learn something new and the experiencing of those newfound skills make up the appeal for this sport.

Training-monotony is a phrase the skater does not know. Whenever skateboarding has tended to imitate other sporting events like the slalom or high-jump, that maneuver has rapidly lost its appeal with the result that such activities play only a minor role in the overall sport of skateboarding.

Important, also, is the fact that a skater does not have a "trainer" but is one's own boss. This eliminates conflict that could otherwise dampen the fun. Learning usually takes place in the company of other enthusiasts and the skaters motivate each other. This fosters a healthy rivalry, one that is challenging rather than divisive.

But the good athletic strenuous activity is only one side of skateboarding. As mentioned, the skateboard is also a mode of transportation that has proven to be very popular, particularly for short distances. Of course, there may be more comfortable and faster ways of getting from point A to point B, but none is more exciting. And none allows a person to have so many new experiences, learn new skills on the way, and have so much fun in the process. Nothing will stand in the way of skaters having a good time, as long as they behave responsibly, which means not trying to jump over cars or skate too close to display windows, are considerate and careful not to startle passersby. Of course, some will insist that that's just what makes skateboarding so much fun, certainly a sign of a hefty case of youthful rebelliousness and immaturity. Too, perhaps some skaters feel they have to live up to a reputation. One of being a bit crazy, defiant, and different maybe?

Okay, so now we are getting around to the skateboarder's lifestyle. To understand the character of skateboarding and the lifestyle con-

nected with it, let's take a look at how this sport developed.

Skateboarding has always been seen as a traffic hazard, so laws were set up regulating or banning it. Since it was and still is illegal in many places, skaters often are, in fact, "lawbreakers." In addition, spectators considered skating, particularly tricks in the halfpipe or pool, as extremely dangerous. These two factors, illegal on the one hand and health hazard on the other, gave skating its notoriety in the eyes of the public. Skateboarders were forced to become the reckless outsiders of society. Of course, since this image only reinforced young people's sense of belonging, many began to identify with the sport. Skating is one way of expressing rebellion, for instance against one's parents, without creating too much conflict. The fact that skating has no preconceived rules fits the need perfectly.

Industry did not

fail to exploit this image in its marketing strategies. The music industry quickly made rock music part of the skateboarding scene, serving to give skaters an additional means of identification. Specially designed T-shirts followed. Now one could make a statement even outside of the skatepark or pool. But skateboarding can also be described very easily by using the following formula: Skateboarding = fun + freedom.

This book covers the three most popular phases of skateboarding: freestyle, streetstyle, and halfpipe or vertical skating. The skater who has never been on a

skateboard will learn the basic positions with the help of the chapter, "Let's Skate." For the sake of clarity, the three disciplines are introduced and discussed separately. The explanatory text will also describe the particular protective gear needed for each discipline. Please pay close attention, because it is here we will point out important points of safety. We want to make it clear to the reader that skateboarding is *not* a risk-free sport, and the danger of injury is not small. But risks can be kept to a minimum if protective gear is worn and if the skater learns, right from the start, how to "fall."

Claus Grabke

HISTORY

*A lot has happened
in a short time.*

Sometime during the late fifties, a few California surfers got the idea of mounting axles and wheels from roller skates onto a wooden board. They wanted to find a way to duplicate the sequence of movements they used in surfing on the pavement. It was the birth of the "asphalt surfer."

While the asphalt-surfing board did give rise to thoughts of skateboarding as a serious sport, it wasn't until 1962 that skateboarding became established and *the skateboard* was born. The news immediately sparked a skateboarding boom even though no skateboard industry even existed at that time. Skateboards were not mass-produced until 1964, when manufacturers, such as Hobi and Makaha, began to fill the needs and reap the financial benefits of the new sport. That year also saw the first publication of *Skateboarder Magazine*.

The first international competition took place in 1965 in Anaheim, California. Two disciplines, freestyle and slalom, were featured. It was at this contest that the most distinguished competitive skater of the sixties and seventies was discovered, although he was not among the winners. His name: Bruce Logan.

Unfortunately, 1965 was also the year skateboarding was confronted with a problem that has continued to plague it to this day: illegality. Cities and towns all across America started to issue ordinances that prohibited skateboarding on public streets, roads, and in shopping malls. Skaters were forced to look for alternative places, away from public areas, to enjoy their new-found sport. When they discovered round, empty and abandoned swimming pools in their neighborhoods, a new and exciting dimension was introduced to skateboarding: vertical skating. In spite of this promising development, stagnation set in and for several years skateboarding became an activity plied by a few determined insiders only.

In 1972, however, skateboarding began to reawaken thanks, largely, to the efforts of Frank Nasworthy, who discovered and invented the urethane wheel for the skateboard. This urethane wheel revolutionized skateboarding. It made skating faster, opened the door to new and more challenging tricks, and made skating much more comfortable.

By 1975, almost all of America seemed to be standing on skateboards and manufacturers began to sponsor and pay individual skaters. It was the birth of the professional skateboarder. Tony Alva, Tom Sims, Stacy Peralta, and Jay Adams were some of the skaters elevated to pro status. Skateboarding began to spread throughout the world. In no time, countless new enthusiasts found themselves suddenly on skateboards and, shortly thereafter, in hospital beds.

In 1976, as the wave of skateboard hysteria continued to move through the byways of the United States, skateboard parks began to appear almost overnight. Unfortunately, it seemed that the companies who built them were determined to simply cover a large a surface as possible as fast as possible. The result was that the skating parks were poorly designed and did not do justice to the needs of the

Slalom ramp at First International Competition in Anaheim, California.

forefront and did so with extraordinary speed.

That year saw the invention of the "rock 'n' roll" (the "father" of all lip tricks). In addition, Bobby Valdez invented the inverted handplant, later simply called the invert. These acrobatic stunts enriched the sport tremendously.

Another new refinement was developed in 1977. Jim Muir and Wes Humpstone, both representing Dog Town, asked the manufacturer to design wider boards. Up until then, the standard board measured about 7½ inches (19 centimeters). At first, people just grinned when they saw the "pigs," as these wide boards were called at the time. But it didn't take long for skaters to realize that the increase in width had many advantages.

In 1978, a skater from Florida arrived in California and reshaped skating. He invented a trick that remains to this day a

skaters. The following year, while Tony Alva won the world championship of professional skateboarders, the skating world saw the birth of what can only be described as the Mecca of Skate-boarding. The skatepark in Upland, California, opened its gates in the fall of 1977. The builder of Upland Skatepark, sparing no expense, designed a park that continues to excite skaters to this day.

Other equally well-built parks, like Marina del Ray, Del Mar, Oasis, and Winchester, followed in short succession. Skaters wasted no time in using these parks to push vertical skating to the favorite of everyone, particularly beginners. The name of the skater is Alan "Ollie" Gelfand and the new move was called the "ollie air." In the beginning, Alan used his new technique for the then so-called no-hand air in the vertical, but later he included it for jumps on the ground. It was now possible to jump over low barriers, like the curb of a sidewalk. This trick opened up a whole new style of street skating.

Now came a time of experimentation, when skaters had fun inventing new moves, a trend that continued throughout the following year. Some of the experts, among them Alva, Bowman, Caballero, Miller, McGill, and Peters, to name just a few, came up with new tricks with breathtaking speed. Eddie Elguera's frontside rock 'n' roll, the miller flip invented by Darrel Miller, and the frontside air variel invented by Eric Grisham deserve special mention.

In the summer of 1980, Alan Gelfand and Stacy Peralta signed up as trainers at camps opened up in Sweden specifi-cally for skateboarders. The camps became a real institution on the skating scene in Europe. But while great progress continued to be made in the technique of skating in the new decade, the number of skateboarders worldwide began to decrease. Again, one could sense that a crisis was in the making. In 1981, *Skateboarder Magazine* published its last issue, and skateparks began to close down due to a lack of skaters, Soon only small groups of diehard enthusiasts remained. Among them, however, were the superstars of today, lead by Tony Hawk and Christian Hosoi.

Over the next four years, skateboarding remained in something of a vegetative state, kept alive only by skate videos and the determination of a select few who would not let go of their favorite sport. Finally, it paid off. In 1985, a new boom began. The midwives of this third, big explosion were not new techniques but the already well-known wooden half-pipes and the ollie.

Upland Skatepark

THE BOARD

To some, it means everything!

While manufacturers do make skateboard parts of high quality that allow professional skaters to custombuild their own boards, skateboards practically ready for use are easily available. These are recommended for beginners or those just starting out who want to get a feel for the sport but have yet to make a serious commitment. The top price of $170 for a professional board might be more than a beginner is willing to pay. At the other end, ready-made boards are available for as little as $30, but the material is inferior and the construction does not incorporate all that technology has to offer. Also, they are too heavy, a decided disadvantage during the learning process.

Experienced skaters generally build their own boards, choosing the surface coverage, axle, and wheels according to the style of skating they intend to pursue. In addition, skaters then choose accessories, colors, and grip tapes that both express their individuality and assure them that their board is uniquely their own. And skaters *are* individualists! Each skater develops a close personal bond with the board selected and sees skateboarding as not just a sport but a calling that is shaping his or her life and environment.

Skateboard decks for street, ramp, and freestyle skating

14

The Deck

Given the endless variety of skateboard decks on the market, it is difficult to give an overall view. However, they all have one thing in common. Regardless of the make, they all consist of seven

maple wood possesses.

Depending on what type of skating a board is to be used for, requirements vary for each deck: in the degree of concavity, with either one or two upright bends, and in the

length of the nose and tail. The overall size of a board also influences its maneuverability. The concave curve (see diagram) was designed to allow the skater to stand more

securely on the board and provide support for the feet. But the differences serve another function. The degree of a bend, for instance

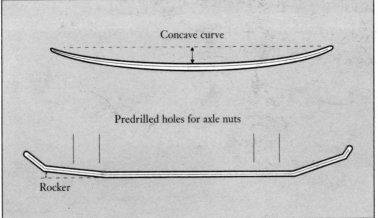

Cross-section views of width (top) and length (bottom) of a deck

layers of maple wood glued together under heat and pressure so that the grain runs vertical for two layers, and horizontal for five layers. This construction increases the already considerable strength

Concave curve

Predrilled holes for axle nuts

Rocker

15

in the back, called the kicktail, determines how far the front end of the deck, called the nose, will lift off the ground. This is an advantage for the Ollie trick, because here the degree to which the nose comes off the ground is an important factor. On the other hand, the kicktail also presents a disadvantage because the foot, positioned on the tail, is more severely bent at the ankle.

The nose of the modern board is shaped much like the tail. In the past the nose, extending only slightly beyond the front axle, was very short and pointed. It was thought that this would give the board a more sleek appearance. Today, however, the nose as well as the tail, are integral parts of the performance of many stunts. The nose is, therefore, wider and bent upwards, to allow the skater a good grip on the board.

The width of the board should be chosen according to the skater's shoe size. A board that is too wide does not give the skater a good sense of the board below him, because his toes as well as his heel cannot get a feel for the edge of the board.

The distance between the two axle nuts, as well as the geometry of the axle (see diagram on opposite page), are of prime importance for the maneuverability of the skateboard. If the distance is wider, with all other dimensions being the same, the board will have a wider turning radius.

Some decks, particularly those for streetstyle skating, are designed with the bend at the nose already beginning at the front axle (see diagram). This portion, called the rocker, also influences the steering ability of the skateboard. The steeper the "rocker," the steeper the position of the pivot of the axle and the more

agile the board will be (see axle diagram on opposite page). This angle will balance out a possible disadvantage created when the distance between the axle nuts is wider than normal, making even relatively longer decks more agile.

The dimensions of a deck, therefore, should not overly influence the choice of a skateboard. Much more important are the needs of the individual skater and his style of skating.

The Axle

Axles, also called trucks, are not just parts that connect the rollers to the deck: they are perfectly balanced precision instruments that give steering ability to the skateboard. Since weight is of primary importance, hanger and baseplate are made of aluminum, magnesium and, most recently, a very stable plastic. The axle and the kingpin are made from rust-free steel

that can withstand the extreme stresses created during skating.

On casual observation, very few differences can be detected between the many different models on the market. With closer inspection, however, it is easy to see if an axle will give you good maneuverability or not. The more agile the axle, the tighter the turning radius of a skateboard when compared to one without that design, even if the decks of both have the identical degree of upward bends.

Let's take a closer look at the diagram on page **17**, particularly at the area where the pivot is attached to the baseplate. The steeper the angle of the pivot in relation to the baseplate, the more agile the axle will be and vice versa. Because, when the axle reacts to a steering movement, the hanger turns around the vertical axis of the pivot.

The construction of the axle, the angle of the pivot in relation to the baseplate and consequently the mounting of the kingpin, determines the geometry of the axle. Depending on the skating that is contemplated, a more or less agile axle has its place. When skating down-hill or in a halfpipe, for instance, many skaters prefer a less agile axle, because it gives a more stable and quiet straight-ahead run. By con-trast, more agile axles are called for in slalom and street skating.

The width of the axle together with the mounting of the wheels should always correspond to the width of the deck. The movement of an axle is determined by the degree of strength of the grommets and by the adjustment of the kingpin nut. Each axle has two grom-mets: the inner and the outer. If softer grommets are cho-sen, the axle will re-act to minimum pressure and turn faster. Skaters with less bodyweight need softer grommets; heavier skaters need harder grommets. Fine adjustments are made by tightening or loosening the kingpin nut.

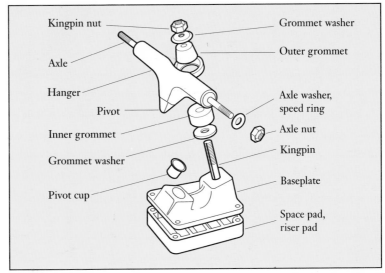

Kingpin nut —
Axle —
Hanger —
Pivot —
Inner grommet —
Grommet washer —
Pivot cup —

— Grommet washer
— Outer grommet
Axle washer, speed ring
— Axle nut
— Kingpin
— Baseplate
Space pad, riser pad

Construction of a skateboard axle

17

The Wheels

Choosing the best wheels for a skateboard depends on what type of skating will be done and by the skating style of the individual skater. Improvements were made by the use of new wheel shapes and by the development of a new material with good rebound ability. Size and shape, next to the degree of strength, are foremost in determining how wheels, and

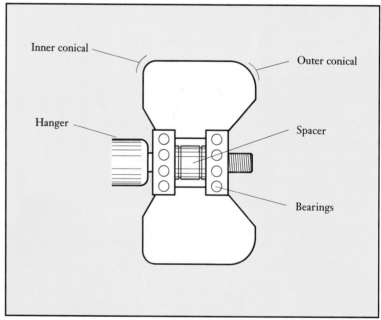

Cross section of a skateboard wheel

consequently a skateboard, will perform.

Wheels with a larger diameter (64mm and more) are generally faster and move better over small stones and other uneven ground than those that are smaller. They are, in addition, preferred for skating the half-pipe precisely because they are faster and allow the skater to reach more "air." Smaller wheels, on the other hand, give better control when doing lip tricks in the pipe and for street skating. The width of the wheels is another point to consider. Although a wide wheel holds to a surface better than a narrower one of equal strength, it will slow the board down, since a wider surface encounters greater resistance.

The conical shape of a wheel refers to the rounded inner or outer edge (see diagram on opposite page). An increased conical results in better maneuverability over small ledges and elevations, while an edge with a decreased conical makes sideway approaches to an obstacle easier. However, a smaller conical also reduces the riding surface.

The degree of strength of most wheels is measured in durameter "A" and is always printed on the wheel. Generally, the strength lies between 80 A and 98 A. Softer wheels (78 A–85 A) run smoother, quieter, and are better in evening out rough surfaces and in "sticking to a surface" than a hard wheel. They are ideal for street skating and skating on uneven terrain. Hard wheels (95 A and above) are always faster and give the skater a better surface contact. A skater that likes to slide needs harder wheels, because they release the surface sooner and more evenly (preventing "lolloping"). Generally, the more even the surface, the harder the wheels should be. This is why very hard wheels are preferred in the halfpipe and when skating in competition. To avoid uneven wear of the wheels, it is best to rotate them often. The most practical rotation is to exchange the right front wheel with the left back wheel and the left front wheel with the right back wheel. However, sooner or later you will have to replace the old, worn-out wheels for new ones.

Small Accessories

The individual needs of a skater determine what kind of accessories will be wanted. The type of skating and personal taste, among other considerations, play an important role. In the meantime skate shops offer a wide variety of accessories.

Those accessories that are directly mounted to the deck are best attached either with regular bolts and nuts purchased from a hardware store (making sure that the necessary holes in the board are predrilled) or with so-called T-nuts available from a skateboard shop. When predrilling the holes, it is important to use the proper bit size. To avoid splintering the layers of wood, make sure that you apply an even, light pressure with the drill held perpendicular to the surface. If the accessories are to be attached with wooden screws, pre-drilling with a very thin bit is also important so that the screw can properly grip the wooden deck. However, wooden screws are not recommended. Large wooden screws put too much pressure on the layers of wood that have been glued together and can force them to separate. Wooden

screws, furthermore, have a tendency to pull out of the board much more easily.

Bearings

We recommend precision bearings that are closed on both sides, since they are maintenance-free. There are, however, differences in price and quality among the available models. Do not skimp when it comes to ball bearings. Those of good quality will perform quietly and smoothly for a long time. It is important to use spacer between the bearings and the wheels, because they will run poorly without it and the bearings will wear out much quicker.

Grip tape

Grip tape, a self-adhesive tape, is a must on every board, because it prevents the skater's feet from slipping. It is offered in every conceivable color, by the yard, and available in every skate shop.

Space pads

Space pads are

mounted between axle and deck to increase the distance between the deck and the wheels. The common sizes are $5/16$ and $9/16$ inches thick and correspond in diameter to the size of the baseplate of the axle. Wedge-shaped space pads also influence to a great degree how a skateboard maneuvers in a turn. Depending on where the thin or thick portion of the wedge is positioned under the pivot, the axle will react either slower or faster to the skater's steering.

Tail saver

The tail saver is mounted under the tail of the skateboard deck. As the name indicates, its only function is to prevent premature wearing-down of the edge of the tail.

Nose saver

The nose saver is a strip attached to the front edge of the deck. It is primarily designed to prevent premature wearing-down of the edge.

Rails

Rails are mounted under the sides of the deck so that the skater can get a better grip on the board and also to allow the board to slide more efficiently when doing tricks, such as the railslide.

Nose rail

The nose rail is a strip attached to the underside of the deck at the nose to give the skater a better grip on the board.

Copers

Copers are mounted to the axle hanger to prevent wearing-down of the axle during certain tricks, like the grinder.

Rip grip

The rip grip is an accessory that comes in many different shapes. It is made either of foam rubber or a rubber material and is mounted on the underside of the deck. It gives the skater a better grip on the board and is mounted wherever the skater will most often hold onto the board.

PROTECTIVE GEAR

Dispense with it at your own risk!

Protection against injuries is a very important subject. The skateboarding industry today provides a great many accessories designed specifically to ensure safe riding, so it's smart to take advantage of it. Those who once chose not to wear protective gear could tell you a long, sad story or two about it. Knee and elbow guards are most important, because these are the parts of the body most vulnerable in case of a crash. The thickness of the cushion varies. The "small," thin ones are good for street skating or freestyle. Skating in the halfpipe requires "big," heavier cushioned pads, like the Rector Fat-Boys or the Pro-Designed. So protected, in case of a fall, the skater can slide "softly" on knees and elbows. "Knee gaskets" or so-called "underpads" are worn under the knee pads, particularly for halfpipe skating. They are important because they keep the knee pads in place even when the skin of the skater becomes wet from perspiration. They are very absorbent and, in addition, give support to the knee

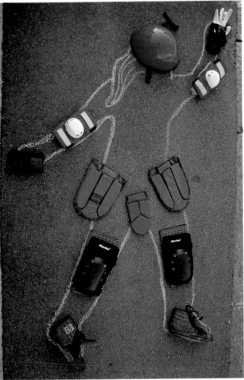

joint, acting like a protective bandage. It is a very good idea to wear a helmet, especially in the pipe. Not only do many halfpipe skaters fall on their heads instead of their knees, but the helmet also protects the skater in case the board should roll beyond the coping and, on its "return trip," land on the skater's head.

Wrists are also subject to injury during a fall, so wrist guards have been developed that stabilize the wrist joint through a built-in plastic brace. They allow for a safe glide which will prevent the hands from being scraped. Gloves are not as popular as they once were, before wrist guards. A skater concerned about hand injuries, however, should not hesitate to use them.

The hip pad is another safety device that belongs to a complete protective system. This pad, made of shock-absorbing material, is worn inside the pants and protects the hip against bruises.

A tail bone guard, made from the same material as the hip guard, is also good protection.

Optimum protection, of course, depends on the proper fit of protective gear: helmet, pads, etc. When purchasing your gear, try on everything to make sure that the size is right and that they make you feel secure and comfortable.

Shoes

Since shoes are first and foremost the connection between the skater and the board, the soles are, therefore, the most important part. They should be made of a strong material that can withstand scraping and scarring. But they should also be soft and pliable so that you have a sufficient "feel" and sense of contact with your board. This, or course, implies that shoes with a heavy profile are not the best choice.

Ollie pads and skins are characteristic of shoe accessories made specifically for skateboarding.

Ollie pads are small reinforcements attached to the outside of the shoe where the greatest stress is applied during the ollie. Skins are the leather flaps covering the shoelaces. They are intended to protect the shoe tips and laces during a slide down the pipe or when performing the impossible trick or the casper during freestyle skating.

It is possible to further protect your shoes by putting adhesive bandages or

In this type of situation, good protection is the best insurance.

tape on critical areas. Too, shoes should be made of leather and should reach above the ankle. In the past many injuries to the ankle and tendons were due to the skater not wearing the proper footwear.

The condition of the terrain is, next to the choice of board and accessories, the most important consideration for skateboarding. This chapter is meant as a guide to finding the almost unlimited possibilities that exist.

Street

The street constitutes a terrain that constantly changes

TERRAIN
*The world is
your sports arena.*

With all the fun you can have while skating, remember that you are not alone in the world! Places where you and other skaters could be endangered, or could be considered an annoyance to others, should be taboo!

its face, due to the different surface coverings. You may glide over smooth or very rough asphalt or ride over cement squares and bump over its seams. Uneven surfaces may conceal obstacles that may cause a fall. Small stones are just as likely to lock your wheels as are grooves in a surface. Roads that are not much frequented by cars are ideal for downhill skating.

Large, flat surfaces, like ice rinks in the summer or empty parking lots, are ideal for freestyle skating or for setting up street obstacles.

Curbs

A curb is any type of elevation suitable for street tricks. A sidewalk curb, steps, retaining wall, flowerbed boarder, as well as cement railing are considered curbs. Cement, painted curbs, steel, and marble can be counted among the "fast" surfaces. Skating them is a lot of fun. Wood, like park benches, is good for sliding but not for grinding. To skate on rainy days, look

for those areas of a park that are covered.

There are, also, other places than streetside curbs for skating, like steps and banks along canals or waterways.

Banks

A bank is any kind of slope; it does not matter if it is curved or straight. Depending on the angle, a slope is either steep or shallow. Excellent are those with an edge at the top that allows the skater to do lip tricks. The surface of a bank can be as varied as that on the street: clinker or cement is ideal, but cement-slab coverings and flagstone

Banks

are also skateable. If the embankment seems to be too steep for lip tricks, try wall rides.

Ditch

A ditch, while not designed for skateboarding, is nevertheless ideal for carving. A "ditch" can be anything from two banks that are opposite each other to an empty water fountain, a dry

Curb, with banks in the background

riverbed, a drainage channel, or a water conduit. Ditches are primarily made of cement and sometimes the surface is sealed. Only visual inspection will tell you if a "ditch" is really a transition (quarterpipe) or is simply a slope. The upper edge can be anything from a simple border to a rounded perfect lip.

Street Obstacles

Some street obstacles are obvious

when you know what to look for. Already existing obstacles are, for instance, park benches, sandboxes, and metal lawn guards. Other obstacles can be created by modifying what is already there. Obstacles may consist of items that have been carelessly abandoned and only need to be moved into proper position to become useable for skateboarding. Too, those who are handy can create their own street ramps, their only limitations being the extent of their carpentry skills. If you want to build your own ramp, decide whether you want a jump or a lip-trick ramp, and look for plans at skateboarding outlets or advertised in specialty publications.

Halfpipe

In the seventies, a halfpipe usually meant simply a cement pipe cut in half. Most of the time it was without a

platform, called the table. It was not until some time later that the table became a necessity. Although the basic design remains the same, a halfpipe conforming to today's standard must fulfill several requirements. Between the two side transitions (quarterpipes) must be a level surface from 8 to 15 feet (3 to 5 meters) in length, called the flat. The radius of a transition should be between 6 to 10½ feet (2 to 3½ meters). The upper portion is vertical, called the vert. At the upper edge of the vert is a pipe about 1½ to 2 inches (4 to 8 centimeters) thick, called the coping, which extends about ¼ inch (½ centimeter) beyond the edge. Behind the coping is the platform called the table.

If desired, extras can be added to this basic construction of a halfpipe. A vertical extension, for instance, can be added on top of the existing vert and fitted with a coping at the

Ditch

Miniramp, with jumpramp in the foreground

Halfpipe

upper edge. An "elevator" is a piece of coping shaped to serve as a bridge between the normal coping and the extension. In the past, halfpipes used to have canyons. They were commonly used as drop ins and as obstacles for air tricks. Today, airs are so high that canyons would be considered a hindrance. If a halfpipe is exposed to the elements, it is important that it have the proper surface, one that withstands bad weather, does not slow down the skater, or becomes slippery when wet. Screen-reinforced cement or sheets of beechwood are good surfaces and are used quite frequently.

does not have a vert. Other than size, the mini is identical to a normal halfpipe, with coping, table, flat and transitions, and a good surface cover. Since miniramps have gained in popularity, people have come up with all kinds of extras. A spine is made by joining two miniramps, eliminating the table, and adding a coping that consists of two pipes welded together. One can create a whole landscape with a spine, a vertical wall, extensions, and elevators. As the miniramp developed over time, a few tricks were invented specifically for it. Since 1990, quite a few competitions have included mini-

ramp skating as a separate discipline.

Skatepark Pool

All the elements mentioned so far that make up a skating environment can be found in a skatepark. They either contain perfect examples of them or have objects, originally intended for something other than skating, serving as obstacles. Regardless of what you find in a skatepark, to skate in one is an experience. Obstacles in a park specifically designed for skating may be somewhat tame, being composed of old wooden structures or, as was the style in the seventies, made exclusively with cement.

The use of wood in constructing later skatepark pools was influenced by the fact that, in the past, skateboard facilities were a collection of different snakeruns ending in a pool. Today's skateparks, however, usually consist of several large halfpipes, miniramps, and a streetskating area. Facilities with so-called tame obstacles, with gentle slopes and banks covered with smooth cement surfaces where a skater does more pushing than riding, are now difficult to find.

Miniramp

A miniramp, also called fun-ramp, is a miniature version of a halfpipe. The height of the ramp is between 1½ and 6 feet and it usually

Münster Bowl

Florian Böhm doing rock 'n' roll in Upland Skatepark.

LET'S SKATE

Basic techniques for every skater.

Before the future skater "steps onto a board," a few words about warm-ups. Skateboarding is a hard sport, where much is asked of muscles, tendons, and joints. For that reason, a warm-up, consisting of stretching and limbering-up exercises with emphasis on the joints, must be considered a necessity. Only "warm" muscles, joints, and tendons are flexible enough to do what you will be asking them to do, so a good warm-up reduces the chance of injury and the danger of sustaining permanent damage.

All right! Taking a skateboard with an average axles adjustment, let's look for a place away from traffic that has an asphalt or smooth cement surface. Check for small stones and similar obstacles that could cause the wheels of the skateboard to become blocked.

A curve or turn is accomplished by simply shifting your body weight, either to the left or the right of the long side of the board, depending on the direction you want to go (see photo). This is one of the fundamental principles of skateboarding. It is very easy to do and you will find moving so effortlessly already a lot of fun. Make sure from the start, however, that your body weight rests somewhat more over your front leg rather than your back one in order to avoid leaning backwards, which can very quickly result in a fall.

Now, without pushing, step on the board, first with the front, then with the back leg. It is important that both legs be positioned over their respective axle, with the weight of the body directly over the middle of the board. Shift your weight slightly and you get an idea of what steering feels like. As soon as it feels safe, start pushing with your back leg while the front leg is pointing in the direction of your ride. After a few pushing steps, set the back leg on the board and let the board glide gently on its own. This "cruising," during which you continue to push every time the board slows down, should be practised well in the beginning so that you get a feeling for proper body posture and balance. Remain skating in a comfortable position on the board, making sure that the back leg does not move too far towards the tail, since that can cause the board to kick up and make you lose your balance.

During this practice session, it will have already become clear whether you prefer the regular foot position or the goofyfoot position. Most skaters, of course, use the regular foot position, with the toes pointing in the direction of the ride and slightly to the right.

Regular foot position

Goofyfoot position

The goofyfoot position is when the toes point instead to the left. In either position, it is possible to push with the front as well as the back leg. Of course, it is much easier to use the back leg, leaving the front leg positioned over the axle (see photo).

The easiest way to stop is to simply step off the board, after having first reduced the speed somewhat, first with the back and then the front leg. The important thing to remember is to always do this in the direction of the ride in order to avoid stumbling or, worse yet, falling. Another possibility for braking is to raise the front portion of the board, at any time during the ride, and let the tail drag over the pavement. However, this wheelie-stop technique (see photo) should only be used if the board has a tail saver in place to avoid premature wear of the deck.

With enough experience on the skateboard, and when the skater feels ready, some of the following maneuvers can be employed to increase speed. The most common method is "jetting" or "tick-tacking." This technique works as well during a ride as it does from a stand. The maneuver is performed by pushing the front axle off the ground, turning 30° with a swift twist, immediately lowering the front to the ground (to stop the process), and repeating it in the opposite direction. These continuous kickturns, executed with swiftness, increases the speed of the board without any pushing on the part of the skater. Another variation is "pumping," a method used primarily by slalom skaters. With a soft axle adjustment, the momentum is increased by swiftly moving the knees from side to side. It is best to practise pumping on a surface with a slight decline. Experts, however, are able with this method to also ride up an incline.

Don't overestimate your abilities when starting out, and try to keep your speed under control. It is also a good idea in the beginning to wear gloves, since falling off the board during this learning phase is almost a given.

Pushing

Backside curve

Frontside curve

Wheelie stop

STREETSTYLE

Skating that can be done anywhere—well, almost anywhere.

Street skating is by far the most natural form of skateboarding, since the skateboard is not only sports gear but also an ideal means of travelling short distances. Unfortunately, the street, with all its hidden skating possibilities, could easily tempt one to declare every city or town a play area for skateboarding. When skating strictly for commuting, however, the ollie method is perfect for maneuvering curbs and other obstacles. This trick, which seems to defy the law of gravity, should be practised and perfected as soon as possible because it is the entrance to many, if not most, of the styles of street skating in addition to simply maneuvering curbs.

With a skateboard under your feet you are in for a fantastic riding experience. In the process, you will learn tricks and develop a keen eye for the many ideal spots for skating that modern architecture affords the skater of today. The downside of street skating is the ever-present danger of painful scrapes and, with the increasing degree of difficulty of the tricks, the possibility of injuring tendons. In the United States, for some street skating competitions the use of protective gear has become mandatory. This regulation makes so much sense that it should be heeded, too, for all general skating on the road. It will not only decrease injuries but increase the skater's sense of safety on the board. First, try considering protective gear as a requirement. One day, wearing it may become a matter of course, and might well turn out to be the best life insurance you could have.

In closing, we would like to make one more important suggestion. Some cities have already outlawed street skating because people considered it a bother and annoyance, interfering with traffic and other passersby. It is doubtful that this would have come about if skaters had used a bit more diplomacy in the beginning. Many a situation can be rescued, in even the most unlikely places, with friendly behavior and a nice word.

Acid Drop

The acid drop is an absolute "must" in the repertoire of every skater. It is a basic trick and the first we will discuss.

In essence to acid-drop means to jump down from something regardless of height: curbs, park benches, even a garage roof. Courage and know-how will determine how far a skater is willing to go. Drive up to the obstacle in basic position and with sufficient speed. On reaching the obstacle, raise the front of the board up, lifting those wheels off the ground. Drive over the obstacle and, as soon as all wheels are off the ground, flex your knees so that the pressure created helps you keep control of the board. Make sure that your feet are directly over the axles to avoid the board breaking in two on landing. This means that the back foot must be moved forward to the back axle after the tail has been kicked down at the beginning of the "jump phase." Bend your knees to cushion the landing.

Slides are not only necessary for braking, they are also fun to do. A slide, regardless of the kind, requires considerable speed to assure a controlled swerve with subsequent slide. The trick we are discussing here was invented by Ty Page in the seventies.

To initiate the ty slide, skate a slight backside curve, followed by pushing the board forward and shifting the center of gravity rearward. The board will now turn 90° to the direction of the ride, which initiates the slide. During the slide, bring your center of gravity over the middle of the board. If you hesitate during the sliding maneuver, the slide will be cut short; and if the momentum is too strong, you will fall on your back. When the right balance has been achieved, the weight is shifted over the middle of the board and pressure is decreased. Before coming to a halt, the weight is shifted from the heels to the toes, which turns the board around 90°, to continue skating. When skating on banks, the skater may support himself by positioning one hand behind him on the ground; the skater will then slide 180° around his own axis. This is called the bert slide.

The "boneless one" is usually just called the "boneless." It was the most used trick in the eighties but has recently lost some of its appeal. For true street skating, however, the boneless must be learned. It is best to try this trick on a lawn first, because the slightest mistake will cause the board to roll away.

Standing in the basic position, bend your knees and hold the board at frontside. Frontside means with the back hand in front of the back foot at the side of the toes. As soon as you have a good grip on the board, bend your upper body forward. In this position you will be able to lift the front of your front foot off the board without losing your balance. The board remains with both the front and back wheels on the ground. Now, lift the back foot and the board, and jump upwards. When you have reached the highest point in your jump, lower your front foot back on and let go of the board. Land in your basic position, bending your knees to cushion the impact. If you grip the board with the front hand on the front axle where your heel is, the trick is called "bean plant." Using this method, when the board is moved along your back, the trick is called "backside boneless." After you have mastered this trick on the lawn, you may move on to the street, experimenting from a stationary

position and
during a ride. With
the help of the bone-
less many obstacles,
like steps, are no
problem.

Ollie

Without a doubt, the ollie is *the* street skating trick because it is responsible for street skating reaching the high standard that it has achieved in the nineties. The ollie is the basis for an untold number of variations used today. Like the boneless, in the beginning it is best to try the ollie from a stand.

First, your feet must assume the ollie position, front foot in the middle of the board and the ball of the back foot at the outer edge of the tail. Now, bend-

ing your knees, stoop down and lean slightly forward with your upper body and, by pushing hard on the tail with your back foot and reducing pressure on

the board with the front foot, jump up into the air at the same time. Since kicking the tail has already lifted the board a little off the ground, when you jump into the air the front foot guides the board which will, due to the friction between the grip tape and shoe, be lifted upwards. At the highest point, bring the board back into a horizontal position using your front foot. When you land, you are back in your basic position.

It might take you a couple of weeks to master this trick, so don't be discouraged.

Frontside Ollie to 50/50

The ollie 50/50 is one of the primary variations of the ollie, because it can be executed almost anywhere: on park benches, curbs, and fences. The trick allows the skater to do two things: the 50/50 stall, position-ing the board in the middle of the axle on a ledge, or the 50/50 grind, where the axle is sliding/grinding on a ledge. Start with the 50/50 stall, as it is easier to learn. Then go on to the grind.

At moderate speed, drive up to the curb at a 90° angle. Approximately 8 to 12 inches (20 to

30 centimeters) before you reach the curb, pull an ollie, which should be a little higher than the curb itself. As you push down on the edge of the tail with your back foot, turn your body to the front, similar to a ty slide. This movement turns the board 90°. As soon as the axles are exactly on top of the ledge, push the board down by straightening your legs and the 50/50 stall will land you on the ledge.

The sequence of movements for the grind are the same as for the 50/50 stall except that the speed and the angle as you approach the curve are increased. Important: to avoid injuries, do *not* lean backwards under any circumstances during the landing. After completion of the grind, turn another ollie in a 90° angle to get off the ledge.

Ollie To Tailslide

This trick is a further development of the ollie 50/50 because both require you to execute the ollie technique with a 90° turn. In addition, you must have a good feel for the board in order to initiate the slide.

The skater drives up to the curb in a 45° angle and turns an ollie to land with the tail on the curb. The momentum of the approach is transferred to the tail by leaning *slightly* backwards. To initiate the slide phase, the skater must shift his weight to the middle of the board, and do it as fast as possible. The weight must be centered over the back leg. Towards the end of the slide, the weight is shifted forwards so that the front rollers are again on the surface and, at the same time and before the back wheels touch the ground, the back leg pushes the board into the direction of the ride so as not to lose momentum. As the maneuver is completed, the skater will find his body rather severely twisted; however, a good sense of balance makes up for the seemingly awkward position.

Wallie

To the non-skater, the wallie looks rather spectacular. For the skater, however, it is finally a chance to really let fly. This trick asks the skater to give it one's all, courage and skill, and to know and understand what he is about to do.

The skater, in the basic position, rides towards a wall at a 45° angle and at a relatively high speed. Immediately before reaching the wall, he turns an ollie. Pushed hard with the toes, the skateboard is forced up against the wall in a steep angle so that all four wheels touch the wall. The skater must be leaning backwards as that is the only way the board can be pushed upwards. For support and balance, the front hand touches the wall. At the highest point of the push, the skater shifts all his weight to the back leg so that only the back wheels touch the wall. By turning the upper body towards the back, a kickturn is initiated. This lowers the board. As soon as the wheels touch the ground, the skater must immediately shift his weight back to a normal position or the wall ride will end in disaster.

Fastplant

This rare trick could also be called ollie indy footplant because it is a combination of an ollie and a footplant with an indy grip. However, as the name already implies, the real trick is the speed with which a fastplant is accomplished. It would look awkward and dull if a skater should try the fastplant at slow speed.

For the fastplant, the skater rides in high speed up to an obstacle, for instance the corner of a park bench, and turns an ollie that must be at least as high as the

obstacle. As the board reaches the proper height, the skater's back hand grabs the outer edge of the board right in front of the rear axle and, at the same time, takes his back leg off the board to touch the obstacle. Immediately pushing off of the obstacle, the skater moves his back leg, at the highest point of the jump, back onto the board's tail. The weight of the skater is back over the board, and feet are in the basic, normal position.

4

5

Ollie Nosepick

The ollie nosepick is a further development of the ollie 50/50 and, unfortunately, also more difficult. It is important, therefore, that a skater learn the technique of the ollie to perfection before attempting this new trick.

In ollie position and at a 45° angle, drive up to a curb that is not too high, about 8 inches maximum. Do a 90° ollie that should be a little higher than the obstacle. When the front axle is exactly over the edge, the skater must position himself on top of the obstacle by shifting weight and straightening the front leg while simultaneously

6

pulling up his back leg. The skater will balance himself in this, so-called, nosepick position only briefly, because the ollie nosepick should be performed in one fluid motion. To free oneself from the nosepick, the skater first grabs the board on the front side, jumps an inch or so off the board, and immediately gets back on to return to solid ground. During this jump, which should first be prac-

tised on a flat surface, the weight of the skater must remain centered over the board.

This trick should not be attempted if the curb is too slippery and may make it difficult for the axle to come to a standstill.

The ollie kickflip is one of the most difficult street skating tricks. It is easy to understand why. Contrary to the normal ollie, during the ollie kickflip, the board is turned 360° around its length axis. To learn this trick, the skater must have a good feel for the board and, in addition, a lot of patience, because nobody has ever been able to perform this trick on the first try.

While learning, practise the trick at a standstill. The back foot is in ollie position; the front foot, however, is positioned about 2 inches closer to the heel, about the middle of the board. Follow the basic ollie movement but, at the highest point, with your front foot push the board outward with a light ankle kick. This starts the board turning. Lift your legs up so that the board has enough room to make the turn. After the 360° turn is completed, your feet come back to the board in the basic position. To accomplish this, the skater's feet must be pointed properly and legs must be straightened. When this sequence is mastered, the skater can proceed to practising on a moving board. It is important that the weight of the skater remain balanced over the board to avoid falling.

Ollie Kickflip

In the last few years, the "no comply" trick, introduced by Neil Blender, has given new impetus to street style skating. This trick was instrumental in finally, officially, establishing the freestyle-oriented flatland tricks in competitions. To the casual observer, the trick is similar to the boneless; however, it has more in common with the ollie.

First, the skater rides with his feet in basic position and at normal speed. As shown, see photo sequence, the front leg comes off the board to hit the ground with toes angled upwards. At the same time the back foot, in ollie position, moves forward a little. The board turns in a frontside direc-tion. The board should lightly touch the knee of the back leg to give the skater a better "feel." Now the front leg pushes off the ground, caus-ing the other foot to slide downwards on the board. The board is turned 180° and the body must follow the turn in order to avoid fal-ling. During landing, the skater's center of gravity is again posi-tioned over the board. The skater then continues his ride, but is going in the opposite direction.

No Comply

There are so many variations of air tricks, it is impossible to discuss each of them here. However, all air tricks have two things in common: the approach, and the fact that the skater has a choice of two possible jump-offs.

Sufficient speed during the approach is necessary to assure that the ramp can be cleared safely. Jumping-off can be done in one of two ways. Either the skater holds on to the board during the approach phase and drives over the ramp in this position, or turns an ollie at the edge of the ramp and grabs the board in the air. The first method is recommended for beginners; the second for the skater who has already mastered the ollie technique and who has a very good sense of the board underfoot. The ollie technique makes higher airs possible because the skater is standing erect on the board while driving up the ramp and does not lose momentum by bending over.

Lien air. The front hand grabs the board at the side of the heel.

Method air. The front hand grabs the board at the side of the heel.

Legs are bent at the knees and the board is pulled up.

Rocket air. The front hand grabs the board at the nose and the front foot is placed next to the back one while both legs are straightened.

Jump Ramp Air

180° stalefish. The back hand grabs the board on the side of the heels while the skater makes a 180° turn.

Finding a suitable site, like a wooden or metal plank or, as shown in the photo sequence, a painted curb, is the most important factor in doing this slide. The approach speed will depend on the material and condition of the skater's board as well as the place chosen for the slide. For a board without rails, the speed can be higher than for a board with rails. Judging the proper speed is a matter of experience; one must develop a feeling for it. For instance, a slide on a wooden surface is considerably slower than one done on metal or plastic.

Make your approach in basic position, with the back towards the slide and the board parallel to it. By lifting the front axle and subsequently making a 90° turn, the board is brought into the sliding position and the skater proceeds to slide. In order to remain on the board during the slide, the skater shifts his weight towards the nose of the board so that it is evenly divided between both legs with the center of gravity directly over the center of the board. The change back from slide to normal ride requires that, as the back wheels touch the ground, the board is simultaneously turned 90° to the backside, by pushing on the front axle, to bring the front wheels to the ground facing forward. The railslide can also be done from the frontside, meaning that the skater faces the slide site at the approach and the slide itself is done facing rearwards. This maneuver, however, increases the trick's level of difficulty and requires more feel for the slide and better balance.

Railslide

This trick requires much experience in railsliding on metal and an exceptional and perfect mastery of the ollie technique. Beginners are implored not to attempt this trick, as the possibility of serious injury is enormous.

In order to practise, look for a rail that is not too high and has plenty of room for both the approach and the landing. With your feet in ollie position, gather sufficient speed and approach the rail at a 45° angle. Just before reaching the steps, turn a high ollie and land on the handrail at the center of the board . . . and off you go! Of course, the weight of the skater's body *must* be positioned over the board. Balance is easy to maintain by bending the knees and thrusting both arms out to the sides. The actual slide can be very, very short. At the end, while the board is sliding all by itself on the rail, make a 90° turn and bend knees to cushion the landing, then continue on your way.

Ollie Handrail

HALFPIPE

Thrills, tensio
tremendous physic

One of the most extreme, and surely the most spectacular, forms of skating is to ride the halfpipe. It is here that the skater can overcome, if only for a brief moment, the force of gravity and "fly" in a seemingly weightless state. The height of the halfpipe alone causes an uneasy sensation in the stomach and the performance of the tricks provokes a high output of adrenalin. It is no wonder that this discipline attracts skaters like a magnet. The fascination, for the expert, is in direct relationship to the difficulty that this skating presents to the beginner. The skater about to ride the halfpipe must bring to this feat a healthy portion of courage and must be in good physical condition. It goes without saying that such skaters must also be accomplished in streetstyle and must possess a good feel for the board. In addition, unlike other disciplines, moments of accomplishment are hard to achieve in the beginning.

Actual vertical skating begins with the drop in and with simple lip tricks. Learning them, however, may take weeks. Skaters new to the halfpipe must keep that in mind and should not be discouraged when successes in the beginning are few and far between. Falling down is a common occurrence and part of the game. Nobody, not even the most accomplished skater, can do these tricks at first try. That's why "crashes" have to be taken in stride. They are the necessary evils encountered on the way to perfection! Because of the height and the unfamiliar sequence of movements involved in skating the halfpipe, however injuries can be quite serious so **wearing protective gear is a must**. Furthermore, before attempting the first trick, **learn how to fall**. As soon as a skater realizes that the attempted trick is not working out, he must take cover. Otherwise, very painful collisions with the board are a certainty. The skater takes cover by either jumping off the board or pushing the board out from under him and falling down on his knees. It is very important to practise this maneuver during the transition period. Suddenly falling down onto the flat can cause serious injuries, while crouching allows the skater to slide on his knee guards. Under no circumstances should the skater try to "run" out of a fall. During a fall the body tries to brace itself and this exerts considerable force on the body which, over time, does damage to the tendons of the ankles, knees, and hip. If a skater heeds these warnings, and acts on them, vertical skating is not nearly as dangerous as it looks and might even be less stressful than street skating with its sometimes nasty surprises.

Tricks for the halfpipe are basically divided into three

groups: lip tricks, hand or foot plants, and airs. Lip tricks are done at the coping and the board does not lose contact with the ramp. During plants, the skater either "plants" a foot on the coping or touches the coping with one hand while the board continues to go over the edge of the ramp. Finally, during airs, the skater jumps over the ramp and totally loses contact with it. These descriptions, however, do not reveal anything about the degree of difficulty involved in any of the tricks. Often lip tricks, which appear to be so easy, are much more difficult than airs, which look much more complicated.

The following chapter will cover the three categories of halfpipe tricks established above in order. We will, however, begin with entrance tricks and maneuvers that must be mastered in order to reach the ramp and execute the tricks.

Taking Off, Fakie and Pushing

The first step in the halfpipe consists of skating from one transition to the other without turning. Skating both forwards up the transition and backwards skating down are called "fakie." To achieve this "pendulum movement," the skater must push to achieve a certain momentum. The pendulum motion is done in one of two ways: a skater can either push while standing in the flat or run up a transition and jump on the board. The first method is the easier one, but it does not give the skater much momentum. Also, it is not useful on halfpipes with a short flat, so it is best to try to learn the sec-

ond method: jumping on the board on the transition.

Hold the board at the tail and, while running up, push it ahead of you. When you are up high

enough, jump on the board with both feet at the same time, or almost simultaneously. The process can be made easier by placing one foot on the board just a heartbeat before the other.

In the beginning, do not try to run too high up the transition. Starting at a lower point makes it much easier and you will learn faster. After the skater is on the board and riding down the transition in forward position, he must put all of his weight forcefully on the board and release it when riding up on the other side. This is called "pushing." Anyone who has ever sat on a swing and "pumped" will have no problem understanding this principle. When the opposite side is reached, the whole process is repeated, with the skater now riding down in the backwards position. It is important that the skater look in the direction of the ride, to start pushing at the proper moment.

The kickturn, as such, is not a trick in the strictest sense of the word. Rather it is a combination of movements, continuing where the fakie leaves off, which allows the skater to ride up to the coping.

To perform the kickturn, ride up the transition to the point where the turn is to be executed. Here shift your weight to the back leg to allow the front wheels to lift off the surface. Then, prepare for turning by pushing down on the board with the ball of the back foot and, at the same time, turn your chest to face the flat. This is the only difficult phase. The skater must make sure that his body is in alignment with the board. Two mistakes are often observed at this point: a skater first turns the board and then his body, or the skater turns his body so fast that the board cannot follow. Both mistakes are potentially dangerous because, in both cases, the front foot may slide off the board. If a skater becomes aware that he is making either or both of these mistakes, he can work on correcting it by crouching and looking down at the board during the turn. After the board has been turned, the skater's weight is shifted back evenly to both legs and the ride down the transition continues.

Backside Kickturn

Tips

★ Riding the turn similarly to riding a curve makes it easier to maintain balance.

★ A skater who has difficulty standing on the board can hold on to the board at the nose with the front hand.

★ While turning, the skater must not straighten up. Rather, the body must remain in a 90° angle to the transition.

Drop In

For the beginner, the drop in is quite a challenge and represents considerable risk. But it must be mastered if serious skating in the half-pipe is the goal. In reality, the drop in is quite simple. Anybody who can perform the fakie can also do the drop in, but the problem is fear. This, not insufficient technique, is the main reason for crashes. Therefore, the state of mind for the drop in should be the same as for any other trick: stay cool, take heart, and simply do it!

First, drive the board forwards to tail the coping and make sure that the back wheels are resting against it. Then step on the tail with the back leg, shifting all of the body weight to this leg. Next, place the front leg on the board without putting any weight on it. Now, the deciding phase! Practically all that

you have to do is shift your weight forward, to the front leg. Fix your eyes on a point straight ahead on the transition. As soon as all

four wheels are on the ramp, straighten your legs to create enough pressure on the board to stay on the transition.

Tips

★ For the very first try, it helps to crouch down on the board. This has two advantages. First, the head, and therefore the eyes, are at a lower point than when the body is upright. This takes away some of the fear, because subjectively the ramp seems to be closer. Second, this position makes it easier for a skater to maintain balance and avoid leaning too far forwards or backwards.

★ The skater can continue to hold on to the nose while dropping into the transition. This, too, will help to keep the skater securely on the board.

★ Stay calm and do not try to rush by "falling" into the transition, wanting to get it over with. If this happens, the skater will find himself in the flat before his board. This could be a spectacular sight for onlookers, but it is a rather painful situation for the unlucky skater and does nothing to motivate you to continue.

Eric Nash doing frontside smith grind. ☞

Tips

★ During the grind, the board tends to turn rather quickly and can slide out from under the skater. It is important, therefore, not to lose contact with the board. A skater in a deeper crouch is better able to prevent a board from sliding by straightening his body up slightly.

★ Pay particular attention to the front foot. Since no weight is put on this foot during the grind, it can easily slip off the board.

★ The axle adjustment should be on the soft side.

The frontside grind is an old trick that continues to find much favor, particularly when skating pools. Also, while it is not a very difficult trick to learn, the skater nevertheless needs courage and self control, as the danger of flying over the ramp or getting hung up on it is always a possibility.

The skater needs good momentum when riding up the transition. An inch or so below the edge, the frontside turn is initiated by shifting the weight to the back leg and pushing the heel into the board. At the same time, the upper body is turned towards the flat and the eyes are fixed on the coping. As soon as the back axle has moved beyond the coping, the skater pushes the toes of the back foot onto the tail, which raises the back wheels off the ramp. Now the axle starts to slide on the coping. During the grind, the board is turned on the axle by 180°. After the turn is completed, the upper wheels are back on the ramp. This happens immediately, meaning the skater need no longer be afraid that the board will get hung up. Finally, the weight of the body is shifted back over the center of the board and the ride back down the transition begins.

The 50/50 is a very useful trick because it allows the skater to interrupt his ride and prepare himself for the next stunt. Mastering this trick will also make it easier to learn many other tricks, like the 50/50 grind, the pivot stall, and the smith grind.

The skater rides up the ramp and initiates a high backside kickturn. Just before the wheels touch the coping, he raises his upper body slightly and starts to turn. As soon as the back axle touches the coping, the skater stands completely upright and, in a sense, lifts his body beyond, over, the ramp. He looks at the coping and pushes the front axle onto the coping. The skater now assumes a slightly crouched stance, leaning into the ramp. Looking in the direction of the transition, he turns the board towards and into the ramp. After the turn is completed, all four wheels are back on the surface and the board rides down the transition.

Axle Stall (50/50)

The rock 'n' roll is, in essence, the basic lip trick. It is a good way to practise getting onto a ramp and getting used to one that is unfamiliar to the skater. It is also an important trick to

Rock 'n' Roll

Tips

★ Turning is the most difficult part of the rock 'n' roll. Often the skater will fall onto the ramp because the board did not turn. Learning the trick is easier if, in the beginning, the skater whips the board quickly onto the coping, rather than tries to push the front wheels onto the table.

★ If, during the turn, the skater cannot keep control of the board, he must learn to lean back farther. But he must then be alert to the possibility of the back wheels beginning to slide!

know because it exists in many variations and serves as the base for countless others. However, the rock 'n' roll is not an easy trick to master and it is more for the "technician."

If you want to learn it, be aware that more than a few attempts will be required. Again, the motto here is: "patience!"

To begin, approach the transition straight on, not at an angle. Just before reaching the coping, give the tail of the board a slight kick. As soon as the back wheels touch the coping, straighten your front leg and stand upright, leaving the back leg bent. Lean into the ramp. It is important that your center of gravity remain in the ramp. While the board is pushed onto the table, the skater's body is turned to face the flat. Now all of the weight is shifted to the back leg, causing the nose to come off the surface and allowing the board to be turned. The skater leans back slightly in order to keep better control of the board and to prevent the front foot from sliding off of it. During the last phase, the skater straightens up and rides down the transition.

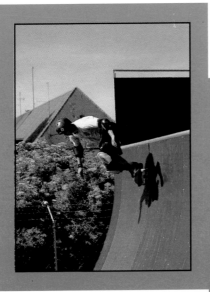

Rock 'n' Roll to Fakie

The rock 'n' roll to fakie is much easier than the rock 'n' roll, but it requires more courage. The trick is to get up enough speed to be able to do the fakie on the opposite side of the transition.

The approach and kick-up to the table is identical to the rock 'n' roll (see instructions on page **71**). But, when the board is pushed down onto the table by straightening the front leg, the skater turns his chest instead towards the table. The weight is then shifted to the back leg, kicking that part of the board down. As soon as the front wheels fall past the coping into the halfpipe, the skater kicks them down on the ramp. Now his weight is balanced equally on both legs and the skater rides down the transition.

Tips

★ In the beginning, do not let the board touch the table, just balance the center of the board on the coping.

★ If you do not feel ready, when first learning, to kick the board over the coping, try to simply ride the front wheels beyond the coping without kicking. Simply give the board a slight push.

Feeble to fakie ☞

Fakie Disaster

The fakie disaster is not a difficult trick to perform, and, therefore, quite easy to learn. Although not very complicated technically, the trick does have its perils, because the back axle can get hung up at any time. Those with limited experience, especially, should not take this trick too lightly, and will need to concentrate well.

To perform the fakie disaster, the skater rides *backwards* up the transition, getting up to the necessary speed with a rock 'n' roll fakie. The "front" foot is placed on the nose. Next, the back wheels of the board are guided beyond the coping without kicking down on the nose. The "back" leg is then straightened and the body leans into the ramp.

Finally, all the

weight of the body is shifted to the front leg, pushing the nose down. The skater, however, should not lean over the ramp too quickly, or it might cause a hang-up of the board. The skater must learn to shift his weight onto the front leg while keeping the body positioned over the coping. Then, while pushing down on the nose, the back foot must be quickly pulled in. This movement will cause the rear axle to flip over the coping. As soon as the skater is sure that the back wheels have cleared the coping, the weight of the body is then shifted rearwards and the front foot is pulled back into the basic position. Now the skater can concentrate on getting up sufficient speed for the next trick.

Tips

★ The skater must try to maneuver the rear axle as far as possible over the coping so that it won't get hung up on the way down.

★ The weight of the body should remain directly over the coping as long as possible; otherwise, the body of the skater will drop past the coping faster than the board.

The feeble grind to fakie is a rather new move that appeared at the end of the eighties, at the same time the lip trick swept the skating world. It is considered to be one of the most difficult lip tricks. A skater must have both, a good sense of speed and excellent technique, if he does not want to "lose his teeth"!

First, the skater approaches and rides up the transition at an angle and at good speed. More speed is required for this trick than for a 50/50. Just prior to the rear axle reaching the coping, the skater turns his chest towards the table. Now the rear axle is pushed onto the coping and the board is turned until the edge touches the coping. While the front leg is straightened out, the body must not be "lifted" off the ramp altogether. The skater must take care that the front wheels are not pushed down on the table, which would prevent the grind. Perform the grind in the position described. In the beginning, it is best to be satisfied with a short distance. During the grind, the weight of the body is on the back leg. While still in the grind, the board is then turned back to the starting position. The weight is shifted off the "back" leg, for a moment, and towards the ramp, to allow the wheels to clear the coping. The skater now places himself firmly over the board and rides *backwards* down the transition.

Tip

★ Wear hip pads,
  and good luck!

77

★ The jump onto the board can be practised without skating onto the coping and without having initiated the turn.

★ As soon as the above-mentioned sequence of movements has been mastered, the skater should practise placing his back foot back onto the board before the tail comes in contact with the coping.

Sweeper

Sweepers, belonging to the category of footplants, do not require much expertise of the skater. The only difficulty is the jump onto the board. One must overcome the tendency to hesitate.

The skater also has to have enough speed or momentum for the board to reach the table.

Before the front wheels hit against the coping, execute a kick and initiate a slight frontside turn by turning the upper body in the proper direction. When the back wheels reach the coping, grab the board's nose with your front hand and step from the board, positioning your back foot on the coping. The board is turned by the front foot, still on the board, turning away from the body and in the direction of the flat. The tail is then set onto the coping, and the upper body follows the turn that was begun by the front foot. When the tail touches the coping, the back foot jumps back onto the board. Now the skater lets go of the nose and does a drop in.

79

Indy air by Steve Claar

McTwist by Christian Hosoi

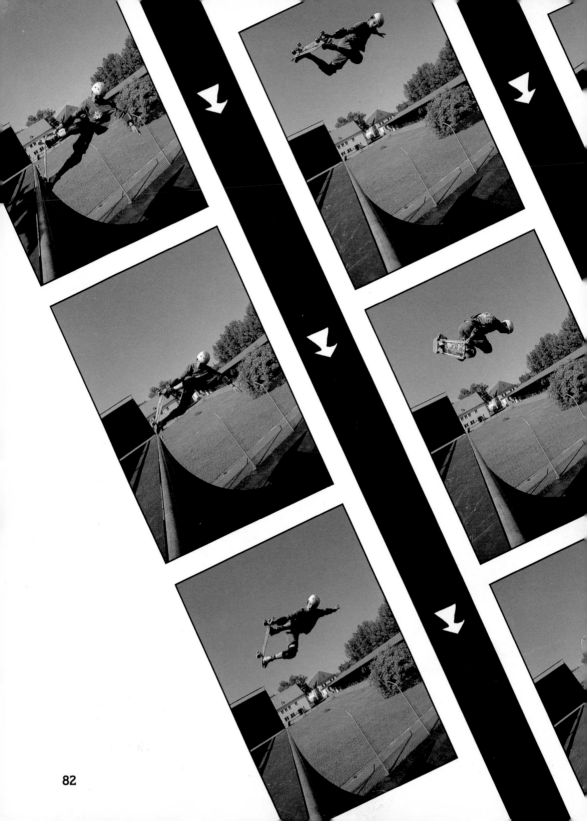

82

Backside Air

The backside air, next to the frontside air, is the father of all airs. It is one of the easier variations and allows the skater the highest jumps. However, the backside air is not an easy trick. Much time and effort must be invested in order to reach anything even resembling perfection.

Just before reaching the coping, the skater kicks the board and straightens the back leg. As soon as the back wheels have touched the coping, the stretch of the back leg is increased. The tail might hit against the coping. The board now moves towards the skater's body. The body remains up-right and the hand quickly reaches for the board after it has cleared the coping. The skater should always grab the board directly in front of the front foot; the result is better control of the board than if it is grabbed at the nose.

Now the body begins the turn, with the back leg pulled up and the board pulled securely against the feet. The skater must make sure, here, that the rear axle has cleared the coping to avoid a hang-up. When the turn is completed, the skater lets go of the board as it passes below the coping and pushes it against the ramp as quickly as possible.

★ The skater must hold his head up when jumping, so as not to lose too much momentum.

★ If the back foot has lost contact with the tail, increase the stretch of the foot as much as possible.

★ In the beginning, practise the air below the coping.

★ The necessary speed can be easily attained with a 50/50 grind or a backside turn.

In very simplified terms, the lien to tail is a sweeper where the back foot is not set on the coping. But the trick is much more complicated than the sweeper, and should only be attempted by experienced skaters.

The skater rides up the ramp at a speed similar to that necessary for the sweeper. Before the back wheels roll over the coping, the front hand grabs the nose of the board and the upper body is turned towards the table. Then the back leg is stretched slightly and the body is brought upright. The skater rides over the coping in this position. Now, as the turn is initiated, it is important to have the body positioned over the board.

Note: pay attention to your "rear end"; it must always be higher than your feet. After the turn, the back leg is straightened and the skater's eyes are turned towards the coping. The tail is pushed forcefully against the coping. After the landing, the body is positioned for a drop in to the ramp and the body is extended.

Tips

★ Don't start the trick too high.

★ It is easier to learn this trick once the tail slide and the fakie ollie to tail have already been mastered.

★ Always try to lean backwards.

★ In case of a fall, try to land *on* the board rather than behind it.

Lien To Tail

Invert

The invert is a preparation for the handplants. Of all of these tricks, it is the easiest to do. In spite of this, it is still very impressive and should be part of the repertoire of a good skater.

The skater rides up the transition at considerable speed. Just prior to reaching the coping, the front hand grabs the inner edge of the board. The other arm is stretched out and the eyes are fixed on the coping. Before it has passed the coping, the board is pulled up and the skater now pushes himself lightly away from the ramp. This is necessary because, experience has shown that during the learning phase, the beginner will not be able to upright his body properly and his center of gravity will, therefore, carry him in the direction of the table (beyond the ramp).

The skater grabs hold of the coping, shifts his weight to the arm holding the coping, and begins to turn backwards. While this is going on, it is important that the board is held tightly against the feet. When the turn is completed the skater, still holding the coping, lets himself fall back towards the ramp, pulling the board slightly towards the supporting arm. As soon as the skater is sure that the board has cleared the coping, he takes his hand off the coping and pushes the board against the ramp.

The frontside handplant is one of the oldest handplant tricks. It is both an impressive trick to watch and a rather complicated one to perform. The skater must be in exceptional physical condition in order to stay in control during this feat.

The skater rides up the transition and grabs the board with his back hand when he is just below the coping. The front arm is stretched out and the eyes are fixed on the coping, while the body leans backwards. In this position, the skater rides beyond the ramp and grabs the coping so that his arm pushes the body straight up into the air. Afterwards, the board is pulled towards the supporting arm. Now, the skater lets go of the coping and, reorienting himself, "falls" back to the ramp.

Tips

★ When doing the handplant, the body must be pushed straight up and come down straight. Trying to move in an arch will result in too wide a turn.

★ The turn must be slowed down at the highest point. This is the best way to avoid an exaggerated turn, and it also eliminates the possibility that the

Frontside Handplant

☞ *Frank Messmann doing invert channel.*

skater will fall on the supporting arm.

FREESTYLE
Board artistry on level ground

Another extreme form of skateboarding is freestyle, where a skater performs, to music and on level ground, as many tricks of his choice as possible. Freestyle skating has recently gained in favor and importance. There are now more freestyle skaters, demonstrations, and competitions than ever before. Freestyle skating can be done anywhere: on the street, in a parking lot, or in a

Rodney Mullen

garage — if necessary, in the smallest of places. Railflips, pogos, impossibles, or flips, it does not matter — spectators see most of these tricks as simply impossible to perform. But magic has nothing to do with it. All that is needed to skate freestyle is patience and practice.

Nobody has done more for freestyle skating than Rodney Mullen. He brought new dimension to freestyle skating in the early eighties and has, as a trendsetter and a favorite among competitors, earned the admiration and respect of freestyle skaters worldwide.

A freestyle board is smaller and lighter than the normal skateboard. This makes it an ideal instrument for performing tricks. Shoes for freestyle skating should support and protect the ankles to keep injuries to a minimum. Leather boots that cover the ankles are, therefore, the best choice.

Furthermore, it is important that the skater does not start out trying to do the more difficult and spectacular tricks first, even if temptation does loom large. It is better to put together, systematically and with increasing confidence, a repertoire of tricks that build on each other. With a good amount of footwork, and making use of other so-called basic tricks, the skater will soon establish a sound foundation from which to grow. Otherwise, efforts are quickly doomed to failure, if the necessary skills and a good sense of the board are missing. The frustration resulting from too much haste can easily be avoided. Too, with a good amount of experience in freestyle skating behind him, the skater will find it much easier to learn the more difficult movement sequences, and a very personal skating style will be established much sooner.

Every new trick learned will increase a skater's enjoyment. Try it, and have fun!

Walk the dog is one of the oldest freestyle movements. This trick belongs, like the end-over, to the category of "footwork." Footwork is an ideal warm-up to freestyle practice, as well as a limbering-up exercise prior to doing a hard trick or routine.

To walk the dog, the front foot is placed in the middle of the deck, toes pointing in the direction of the ride. Weight is primarily concentrated over the ball of the foot. The ball of the back foot is placed on the nose, toes turned towards the inside. Then the board is turned exactly 180°. This sequence of movements is repeated as often as necessary. It is important to remember that the skater, at all times, should be looking straight ahead and that the foot of the front leg must point forwards. Equally important for good balance is to keep the upper body as still as possible.

Walk The Dog

End Overs

These are excellent steps to perform directly before or after the walk the dog. From the basic position, the front leg is turned with the heel towards the nose. The toes point to the middle of the deck and the weight is over the front axle. Then both board and body, simultaneously, turn 180° on the front axle. After the turn is completed, the weight is shifted to the back leg and positioned over the tail. Now the same 180° turn in the same direction is executed on the rear axle. The skater can repeat these movements as often as he or she likes.

Kickflip

A kickflip can consist of one, two, or even three turns of the board along its long axis. The technique, however, is always the same, only the force of the push is different.

During the ride, both feet are placed parallel to each other and in the direction of the ride along the outer edges of the board. The position of the feet on the board is either in the middle or with the heels over the rear axle. With knees slightly bent, the sole of the right foot is pushed into the edge of the board, while the heel re-

4

5

mains on the board. The weight of the body is shifted to the left leg. Now the skater uses both arms to gain momentum for the jump, during which the board is pulled up and turned around its own axis. For the jump-up, this arm movement is particularly important. Most of all, however, the skater must try to jump as straight and as high up as possible, and avoid jumping sideways.

After the board has completed its turn, the skater continues the ride in basic position.

6

No-Hand Pogo

The back foot is positioned on the tail, kicking the board up while the front foot is placed under the front axle. Now the skater jumps off the

board with the back leg while the front foot pulls the board slightly towards the skater. As soon as the board comes upright, the front foot is moved to stand on the rear axle, while the back leg holds the board from the side for stability. In this position, the skater can jump up and down as much as he likes. To complete the trick, the free leg is positioned on the nose to stabilize the board, which is then pushed, with the lower foot, towards the front into a halfturn. The ride can be resumed as soon as all four wheels are back on the ground.

Wheelies

Two-foot nose wheelie

*Nose wheelie
space walk by
Günther Mokulys*

The wheelie is one
of the basic tricks of
the very first skaters.
Wheelies are always
executed with the
board riding on only
one axle, whether
the skater is standing
on one leg or two.
These photographs
show just a few
examples.

*One-wheeler
on the rear axle*

*Shove it
by Pierre André* ☞

Space-walk

This is a relatively difficult movement that can only be accomplished with a very good sense of balance and much practice.

In the basic position, the board is lightly pulled off the rear axle. Simultaneously, the skater rhythmically swings back and forth on two wheels, the front rollers never touching the ground. As the momentum increases, the speed of the board also increases. It is important to support the movements of the legs and the board by twisting the upper body and using the arms for balance.

Rail To Rail

With practice, this movement can also be done during a fast ride or when sudden braking is required.

Both feet are positioned perpendicular to the direction of the ride, directly over both axles. Pushing with the balls of the feet, the board is turned forward by one quarter along the long axis until the feet rest on the rail. The front foot is moved towards the nose of the board until the ball of the foot has reached the nose. The board is now pushed another half turn forward with the ball of the front foot. Now the skater is standing on the other rail. This is the position from which many other rail tricks, like the rail-flip, are executed.

3

4

Railflip

5

6

During this trick, the board will turn twice on its long axis while it is, at the same time, thrown 180° around the short axis.

While on the rail, the ball of the front foot is positioned on the edge of the nose with the toes pointed slightly inward. The knees are bent and the skater's upper body leans forward. At the jump off, the weight of the body is on the front foot.

This causes the board to be kicked on its nose. The skater, jumping up as high and as straight as possible, makes a half frontside turn. During this turn, the board flips over twice. When the board is back on the ground, the skater continues his ride in the basic position.

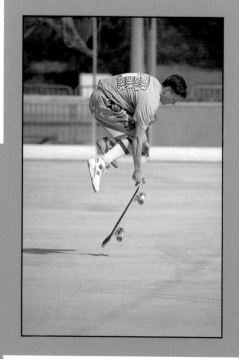

Pogo Fingerflip

The starting point is the pogo, often called the 50/50. Here the skater is jumping on the board which is upright, balancing on the tail. The jumping leg is on the axle, one hand is holding the tip of the board with the thumb pointing down, and the other hand is holding the board by the nose. While do-

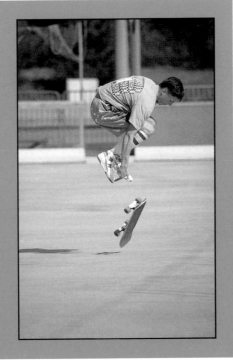

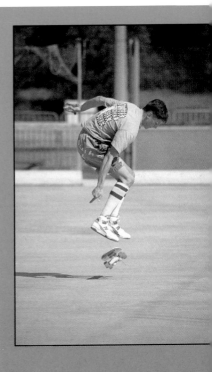

ing these pogo jumps the skater, when high enough, turns the board around with the upper hand and flips it forward. The more upright the board, the easier it is to turn the board around. After one or two turns, the board will land back on the ground and the skater can resume his ride.

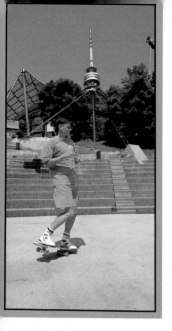

360° Turns

One-wheeler by ☞
Pierre André

There are many different ways for the skater to turn: forwards, backwards, on the front or the rear axle, on one or both legs, and any one of them on only one wheel. Whichever the skater chooses for the 360° turn, he should make sure that it is just the body doing the turning; otherwise he will only succeed in riding in circles and will lose a lot of momentum.

While doing 360° turns, it is important to keep the upper body still and erect in order to keep one's balance. The skater gains momentum by stretching the arms out to each side. During the turn, the arms are slowly pulled back towards the body.

The world record is 127 turns! Rodney Mullen accomplished this unbelievable feat on a board with metal wheels and on hard ground! The average skater will be able to do five to seven turns.

Before attempting this trick, the skater should first have mastered the body position of the flange, as shown in the third photo of this sequence. Both hands hold the board at the tail and nose respectively. Elbows are turned in and pushed tightly to the stomach. The upper body and the head are leaning forward as far as possible and the legs are stretched out and up. Besides needing strong stomach muscles, the flange skater must find and hold the balancing point. With a little practice, this shouldn't be a problem.

During the ride, the skater bends and assumes the starting position. One leg pushes lightly off the board and the skater begins to lean forward with the upper body and the head. In the meantime, the elbows are turned inward and toward the stomach while stretching the legs.

In order to complete the trick, the skater bends the knees and kicks out with a sudden push. The momentum created by this leg movement allows the skater to straighten his arms and bring his feet back on the board.

Flange

Impossible

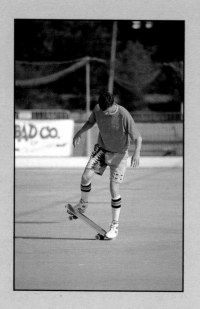

The board is kicked up, and the front foot positioned under the nose. The skater jumps off with

the lower foot while, at the same time, the board is "lifted" vertically with the front foot. The board is turned exclusively with the lower foot, which never loses contact with the board throughout the turn. The trick is to pull the board slightly back during the jump-off and the subsequent turning. When landing, the skater should try to position his back foot as close to the tail as possible.

This trick turns the
board in the oppo-
site direction to the
impossible and
works well during a
fast ride. But, before
attempting this trick,
the skater should
first have mastered
the impossible. With
the board in motion,
both feet are posi-
tioned on the oppo-
site ends of the
board, with the front
foot pointed slightly

in the direction of the ride. The upper body is leaning forward. Both legs are used for the jump-off during which, in addition, the back leg pushes down on the tail and initiates the turning of the board around its vertical axis (see also Impossible). Both feet land back on the board and the skater continues his ride.

Incredible

The incredible is a medium-hard pogo trick and, as soon as the pogo has been mastered, not difficult to learn. First, the skater jumps into the pogo position, which is the starting position for this trick.

The hand that holds the board at the nose throws the board around the foot that has been placed on the axle. The same leg lands on the other axle, while the right, stretched-out hand catches the board. To do the incredible, it is necessary for the skater to jump high and slightly forward. The skater may return to the basic position by doing a pogo fingerflip or any one of the many other possibilities.

Press Kickflip

This trick requires quick footwork. One can barely follow the movement since it takes less than half a second.

The skater stands sideways on the board, with only the toes of the front leg touching the edge of the deck slightly in front of the front axle and the other foot shifted slightly forward. The board is flipped towards

the body due to the pressure created by lightly jumping off with the right foot. Immediately afterward, the right foot kicks the upper edge of the board, making it turn in the opposite direction. The board turns one and one-half times away from the body while the feet are up in the air, after which the skater lands back on the board.

2

3

Handstand Kickflip

1

Initially, the skater should be sure to have mastered the handstand on level ground before attempting to do it on the board.

While in handstand position on the board, the legs are bent at the knees in order to gain momentum. The board is flipped around with both hands after the legs, with a kind of flapping motion, have raised the body off the board. After landing, the skater resumes the ride in the basic position. The movement changing from a handstand back onto the feet should also be practised off the board. It is helpful to think of an imaginary line on which to practise the handstand. After landing, the feet should be back on this imaginary line, which represents the board.

4

5

6

GLOSSARY

A

A: Unit of measurement indicating the degree of hardness of the wheels.

AES: Association of European Skateboarders.

Airs: A group of tricks during which a skater has no contact with the ramp, i.e., is airborne.

Axle: Shaft inside a suspension, with threads on both ends to accommodate the axle nuts.

B

Backside: A move where the board turns in the direction in which the skater's toes are pointing. In the halfpipe, the skater's back is turned towards the coping. See opposite: Frontside.

Bail: 1. Controlled crash. 2. Mistake during a freestyle performance.

Baseplate: Part of skateboard axle containing the suspension.

Basic trick: Easy first move. A trick that every skateboarder should be able to do perfectly.

Bearings: Ballbearings.

Blank: Plain board (piece of wood) before it is shaped into a skateboard deck.

Board: Short for skateboard.

Bowl: Bowl-shaped construction for skateboarding, usually having a flat and a coping.

C

Carving: Skating wide, slalomlike curves; snake runs in the bowl or in the skating pool; skating a snake-run.

Casper: Freestyle trick, with one foot at the front on the underside of the board and the other supporting the board with the instep; logically, the wheels of the board are pointing upwards.

Clay wheel: Predecessor of the urethane wheel.

Concave: Shape of the surface of the board, giving the skater a more secure stand.

Conical: Shape of the outer edge of the wheels.

Coper: Plastic protection of the skateboard axle, attached at the suspension.

Coping: A metal pipe fitted at the edge of a halfpipe vertical. In the past, it was made out of concrete.

Cruising: Relaxed skating on a street, not to do tricks.

Curb: In skateboarding, a sidewalk curb, steps, or any other similar obstacle used when street-skating.

Cushions: Steering grommets.

D

Deck: Skateboard without axles or wheels.

Ditch: Excavation with opposing inclines.

Drop in: Driving into the halfpipe from the table.

Durometer: Measures hardness of wheels, reading indicated on the wheels as A.

E

Elasticity: Sign of quality of skateboard wheels, called rebound.

Elimination: Non-qualification during a competition.

Extension: Vertical addition to a halfpipe.

F

Fakie: Driving backwards down a halfpipe.

Flat: Level portion at the bottom of a halfpipe between transitions.

Flips: Generic term in freestyle skating: turning a skateboard around its length-axis.

Footplant: Any trick where the skater places one foot on the ground or the ramp.

Footwork: Group of freestyle tricks by which the skater moves the board forwards.

Freestyle: Competition on a flat surface without any obstacles.

Frontside: Skater moves in the direction in which his heels are pointing. In the halfpipe, the skater's chest is facing the coping. See: Backside.

Fullpipe: Usually a concrete pipe that allows vertical skating.

Funramp: "Shrunken halfpipe" (halfpipe without the vertical edge) also called "miniramp."

G

Gelfand, Alan: Born in Florida, skated in the late 1970s; invented the "ollie."

Goofyfoot: Leg position on the board, right foot instead of the left toward the front.

Graphic: Design on the underside of the deck.

Grind: Board slides on its axle on the coping or a curb.

Griptape: Rough, sandpaperlike covering on the surface of the board.

Grommets: Firm but flexible axle cushions for steering.

H

Halfpipe: Construction with two curved portions, allowing a skater to drive back and forth.

Handplant: Halfpipe trick in which skater reaches for the coping with one hand.

Hanger: Covering for axle shaft, suspension.

Hang-up: The axle of the board gets hung up at the coping, often the cause of an accident.

Hardcore: Hardcore skater, one allowing no compromises.

Hawk, Tony: The best vert-skater in the world.

I

Invert: Invented by Bobby Valdes, a one-arm handstand in the halfpipe.

J

Jumpramp: Small ramp, usually made of wood, allowing a skater to do jumps.

K

Kick: Upward move.

Kick tail: Back portion (tail) of the board which is bent upwards.

Kickturn: Turning the board by stepping on the kick tail and lifting the front wheels off the ground.

Kingpin: Axle bolt.

Knee gasket: Pad worn under the knee pad (an added protection).

L

Lappers: Accessories mounted at the rear axle to prevent hang-ups.

Lip: Upper edge of the halfpipe, bowls, and skating pools.

Lip tricks: Generic term for tricks performed at the "lip."

M

Maple wood: Very hard wood used to make decks.

Mellow: 1. Half-hearted, as opposed to hardcore, skating. 2. Relaxed lifestyle.

Miniramp: Smaller version of the halfpipe. See: Funramp.

Mullen, Rodney: What Tony Hawk is to the halfpipe, Rodney Mullen is to freestyle: the best.

N

Nose: The front end of a board.

Nosebone: Also nosesaver. Plastic protection for the board nose.

NSA: National Skateboard Association, in America.

N.S.U.: National Skateboard Union, in Germany.

O

Obstacle: Anything that can be used to perform street skating tricks.

Ollie: Skating technique by which skaters lift the board off the ground or the ramp without using their hands.

Ollie pad: Skating glove with a pad reinforcing the outside edge.

P

Pipe: Short for halfpipe.

Pivot: Pin in the suspension.

Pivot cup: Device holding the pivot in the baseplate.

Pool: Empty "swimming pools" with a big advantage: they're round, with no corners or straight surfaces, so ideal for skateboarding.

Pumping: Skating technique to increase speed during slalom.

Pushing: Gaining speed in the halfpipe by shifting weight back and forth.

Q

Quarterpipe: Half of a halfpipe. Much effort is needed to reach edges.

R

Rad, radical: 1. Very risky skating. 2. Particularly breathtaking performance.

Rails: Attached at the underside to hold on to the board.

Rebound: Elasticity of wheels. The higher the rebound, the higher the quality of wheels.

Regular: Basic position on a skateboard, left leg in front of right.

Revert: Following the completion of a turn, the board is turned an additional 180° and the skater skates backwards.

Rip grip: Self-adhesive tape in different shapes for a better grip.

Riser pad: Also, space pad. A pad increasing the distance between deck and axle.

Rocker: A bend in the deck in front of the axle.

S

Shredding: Particularly hard skating; demanding the utmost from both skater and board.

Skatepark: "Amusement park" for skaters, with halfpipes, bowls, snake-runs, obstacles, etc.

Skins: Piece of leather covering shoelaces.

Slam: In contrast to "bail" an uncontrolled crash, usually with painful consequences.

Slide: Wheels skidding across a surface; also on rails or across obstacles.

Snake-run: Slalomlike track with exaggerated curves, usually ending in a bowl.

Space pad: See: Riser pad.

Spacer: Casing connecting inner and outer ballbearing of a wheel.

Speed rings: Washers between hanger and ballbearings and ballbearings and axle nut.

Streetstyle: 1. Skating on the street; strenuous skating including a variety of tricks. 2. Competition of street skaters.

T

Table: Flat portion of halfpipe, beginning at the coping.

Tail: Back of skateboard deck.

Tailbone: Also tailsaver. Plastic protection under the tail.

Tape: Adhesive used to attach protective accessories to shoes after one or several seems to have decided to give up their intended function. (Meaning shoes are about to fall apart!)

T-nut: Flat-headed nuts used to attach small parts to deck.

Transition: Curved portion of a halfpipe, connecting the flat and the coping.

Tricks: "Figure skating" on skateboards.

U

Urethane: Rubberlike plastic used to make wheels.

V

Varial: A group of tricks involving 180° turn of either the body or the board, but not both at the same time. Skater changes position of his feet from goofy-foot position to regular and vice versa.

Vert or vertical: Vertical portion of halfpipe.

W

Wall ride: Driving up a wall (house, building or otherwise).

Wheelie: Group of tricks where the skater skates on one axle only.

INDEX